Mystic Mourn

By Skye Stephenson:

Crystal Companions Cards:
Messages from the Stones and a Star
(card deck/poetry/prose) (2014)

The Spirits of Jade
(novel) (2012)

Ebbo: Offering
(poetry) (2010)

Understanding Spanish-Speaking
South Americans: Bridging Hemispheres
(non-fiction) (2003)

Bounded Evolution
(poetry) (1999)

MYSTIC MOURN

Skye Stephenson

CARNELIAN PRESS

Keene, New Hampshire, USA

Cover photo "Heaven and Earth" by Monica Lee
Cover design by Terry Michael Clark

ISBN: 978-0-9839500-1-1

Published by:

CARNELIAN PRESS
Keene, NH   03431
USA

To Vanessa,
you know who you are,

and

To TMC,
you know why.

CONTENTS

The word Indigenous...does not refer only to people, plant and animals native to an area, but more to a quality that in humans, plants and animals exists as their most original and natural reality before the advent of big civilization...The Indigenous Soul is the Original Soul that is not a human soul, but the natural soul of Indigenous Humans...The Indigenous Souls does not see Nature, but is a part of Nature. Indigenous Soul therefore is not strictly a thing of people only, but belongs to all plants, animals, stars, and places.

Martin Prechtel

A great philosopher-prince named Shotoku Taishi lived in Japan at the turn of the sixth century. He taught, among other things, that one must do psychic work in both the inner and outer worlds. But even more so, he taught tolerance for every human, every creature, and every emotion. The balanced valuing of emotion is certainly an act of self-respect.

Clarissa Pinkola Estes

Mystic Mourn

SPIRIT OF MY SONG

Fly away, fly away, fly away all:
on the wings of a dream,
on the wings of a star.

Take me to
dark nations of
infinite stardust where
rainbows of sounds and
colors liquid collide in the
alchemical mixture of
substance divine.

Wings of
dragon breath:
woven worlds unseen.

Fly away, fly away, fly away all:
on the wings of a dream,
on the spirit of a song.

Thrill
to the thrill
of nothing at all.

Crystal bats, winged caves,
speak to us of gentle days.

Lavender skies, amethyst robes,
Lapis tears
stream from you
and me.

Eyes
of the nighttime,
bleeding and bright.

Soul
of no one
goes into flight.

Sing me those tunes
upon your verdant breast;
Fly me high to the skies
that within me do rest.

Fly me away
on the wings of me;
Let me sing my swan song
on the lagoon of thee.

Fly away, fly away, fly away now:
on the wings of my dreams,
on the spirit of my songs.

MY DAUGHTER'S PAIN

The pain
of my daughter's pain
infuses my brain like a flavored vodkaed drink.

Bubbly and effervescent,
I wallow in her delusions
of what may have happened:
never spoken words
inflected on the
arcs of time.

I know not who I am,
I know not why I came
to inhabit my paltry
heart and brain,
except to say
I love your
shoes.

You sang to me before I knew you
and whispered of what nights are to be.

A weight?
I lift it off.

A family curse?
Perhaps.

The curse of crazy knowingness
no one else would like to hear.

Oh continent wide--
Keeper of the darkest caves, of
Ancestors' bones, cracked and decayed.

While she wonders
who is speaking
ill of her right now--
Perhaps a grandmother
from other times and places
who managed to occupy her brain
and make her go what some call insane.

But I feel not the rot is deep,
the furrows wide,
on caravans of camels' hides.

Maybe she can hide
'til we will all reach the other side.

I embrace my madness
I embrace my lust
I embrace my nothingness
of cinders and dust.

My stay on Earth
it matters not
to anyone
but me,
or so I don't believe
that crosses
crucified happen every day--
some place, some time, new or far away,

are just a symptom, a paltry symptom,
of these so sad and hardened times,
when sweet clinging wisteria vines
weep in a yellow fog
of poppy seeds,
and cherry blossoms wither
on their shriveled vines.

Her hair is still a beautiful
chestnut brown and red,
and down her lovely back
are mariposas blue.

I wish
I never knew
the infinite love
she once awoke in me,
nourishing my deepest needs
of elements and forever seeds.

Oh eternal heart, eternal soul,
perhaps you never grow old,
but I sit here and weep
for the promises
I have yet
to keep.

MYSTIC MOURN I

The pain of the universe
is all around me,
it permeates all I do and see,
it infuses my deepest longings
that prompt me to be free.

Hectare's blade, the iron maid

Worlds whirled--
a marble flung
across the divides
of you and me.

A mystical mourn,
a statistic reborn.

A cauldron,
black and deep,
is my only recourse
when I don't want to sleep.
There with incantations wild
I try to capture for a millisecond
my divine essence, my divine child--
who knows no pain, who is fearless and tough,
who knows how to stand up for herself
and say enough is enough.

And all along trails
of gingerbread cookies divine,
and some drops of blood
(probably mine)--

bleeding from me,
between my two legs
(scrawny and ill-formed)--
maybe one day a new
world will be born.

But for now
alone and adrift,
I long for the distant call
of nothing at all.

Peony dreams,
petaled and white,
shatter my mind
like a stick of dynamite.

Oh bee upon wing
and bird upon lark--

Fly me away,
away from this dark
hole of creation
sucking me down--

fly me away,
away from my hometown--

over mountains and lakes,
across crystal beds wide,
take me on your dreams
to where you reside.

Let me nestle deep
with you when you sleep,

dreaming
our dreams
of a paradise,
simple and true.

Help me steer by the stars
following the winds and the tides
of my birth to the land beyond tides
where the elephants hide
and the beauty of the moment always resides.

Fly me away, fly me away, back to me--
so simple and free.

MYSTIC MOURN II

I was born
on a mystic mo(u)rn:
too big to be pulled from the birth canal

Pearl broke the dam

The withered hand

Corn stalk, tall and proud

Eagle wing

A drop of turquoise
on a rose quartz sky

A crystal cave
where I would hide
when hands came raining down
and there was nowhere else to go but inside.

There I could fly on stainless steel wings,
impermeable to the icy reigns of
Greenwich tides.

The clock chimes nine

The center of gravity
divides our world
into hemispheres,
like our brain.

I

didn't ask to be born
on a mystic morn,
in a frozen land
(parched and bleak)

and

even though I've always
had enough to eat,
the harvest of my people
can't nourish a mystic soul

so

as I grow slowly
old and time
recedes like a smoky
quartz dream,
my crystal
cave's
the only refuge
from a broken world
sprinkled with see-
    men's tears
    and GMO dust.

MYSTICAL MORN

Jerusalem, I sing to you now--
Song of longing, song of lament,
Song of the ancestors yet to be born,
Song of crucifixions of souls
Still being carried out now
In your holy
Name.

Jerusalem, I sing to you of
Justice gone awry, of
Sacred soil so sacrosanct,
Crystallized into coarse
Unleavened bread that
Crumbles and decays
Without a breath of
Fresher days.

O Child of place,
O Place of fair face,
Oh songs of despair
For a place that never was as
Dreams say you may have been
Before the books were
Born.

Threshing floor,
Rock and dome,
Home to no one--
Empty
Soul.

Abraham and David,
Saul and Mohammed too,
Jesus--
Did you truly walk this sacred soil
Long spoiled
By unneeded
Sacrifices of
Blood and
Men?

Woman,
Mother of us all,
Stand tall.

Lift your veil and smile.

Reveal the long sought secret
As we frolic on the hills
And with the daffodills.

Jerusalem, I long for you--
The home I have yet to find,
The mystical morn
Yet to be
Born.

STRIP ME

I want you to strip me
of all my illusions--
true and false.

I want to stand
naked
(front to back)
encased in the honeyed wine
doubly blessed in our communion time.

Make me hurt where I am deep,
ease me from moribund sleeps,
dance with me under moons entwined
where stars sing to us beyond all lifetimes--

On the brooks of days to come,
may we be (just for a moment)
simply and ever one.

And in that grail that burns so bright
I am blinded by your white-winged light.

Save my soul with your song.
Whisper to me, my beloved,
all day and night long.

BARTH - *for James Stephenson (1919-1985)*

I like to think my heart is hard as stone,
cool and glinting, tested by the upheavals of life
and lives to know better than to cry
for personal and planetary histories long gone by.

And yet today I stood by a stone
in a place called Barth
and, truly, cried and cried my heart out.

On those flat and flaxen fields
where now the sun yields
its harvest of pulsating energy divine
that can stream through a machine
and move the pulse of time;
yes, upon those meadowed lands
where these days grey-haired German gents
quietly walk their canine breeds,
giving them some yearned for fresh air--

in those same fields two generations past
sat my father bound by barbed wired vistas
as the Baltic winds raced through his frigid bones
and turned his heart forever into icy stone.

A simple metal plaque placed upon the lonely stone
stands sentinel to all that once existed in that windswept
    land

(Placed there years after my father's too soon death).

Nothing has been forgotten it mutely claims.

But is that truly so?

My father spent a lifetime running from his shadows,
trying to forget a place his fellow compatriots later said
Should never be forgotten.

O my Father dear,
how I wish I could share this memory
gathered today in this solitary space.
All alone I stood and wished you were by my side,
holding my hand, wiping the tears from my eyes;

for this place
(unknown to me until a scant moment ago)
not only haunted you,
                                it has haunted me as well.

It has stalked me as a feline might,
or better put a cobra--
twisting around my soul,
squeezing me unexpectedly,
bringing in the rains and pains
I must have inherited from you,
my courageous father of the artist soul,
who never should have had to go to war.

And I can only wish and pray
that what I did today
may help in some so subtle way
free my own children of the legacies
of wartime degradations
Never to be forgot.

Be free, my son and daughter,
linger long in the sun's regal song
as you let its solar energies erase
any wartime memories etched
from generations past
deep in your innards,
in the innards of your souls.

Let them go,
to be forgotten
like so many things
that ebb and flow in our lives.

And all I can say is that rather than
    Never Forgotten,
Let's strive instead for
        Never Again.

JUNO MUSE

A puff of smoke

You're gone

Loved you
for too long

Be banished now--
Beyond the realm of
Chartreuse.

Bat of my blood
Rises through me,
Carrying the disease
Of eternity.

What did you once know
Before you knew me?

What did you once do
Before you hit me at three?

Shattering worlds with
Fist and surprise--

Velvet
    Hand

Studded glove

You wanted to be my

        --Noose--

        Juno muse
      Shattered smile.

FAIRY TALES

Fairy tale lover and devil man,
who will take my tired and bony hand
and walk me over to paradise
where I can unwind in the glory of me?

Fairy tale dreams and marigold seams,
things are never quite what they seem.

Blue morning glories, birds of paradise too;
cheeky sunflowers, a peony true;
chrysanthemum wings,
cherry blossom heart.

O Unknown one,
please take me too--
to the land unknown
where we can live anew.

I welcome you with a ruby goblet
filled with chartreuse,
fix me a noose, I believe in that too.

If I take ayahuaca
will you fly me high
on the roots of your powers
into the forest divine
to nest with the monkeys
and commune with the trees,
to know the heart of the cobra
and what the elephant hides
in his boneless insides?

Oh I am too weary of all that I see,
just beam me on chemicals
to the land of dreams,
where I never work and everything I want
always comes true--
No lessons learned,
except that I will still be missing you.

Oh celestial designs
that never write fairy tales true--
love begets love in a world made anew,
and on this mystic morn
when I am stillborn,
wet with the dew
I challenge you.

Fairy tale dreams and luscious moonbeams,
chocolate rivers flow over water-
falls of amethyst stars.

Sage smoke, tobacco puffs,
the pipe of peace, sweet grass dust.

Coca leaves
crumble in my hands,
expand my chest, caress my breasts,
while your fingers dipped in the sweet
nectar of the quetzal's embrace
touch the hummingbird's nest.

I call upon the turtle dove song
to guide you along
as you complete your tasks
of milky-wayed passages and maple tree songs,

as your blueberry eyes
and prickly skin
tune
(you and me)
to the beat of the Earth
when it meets the Sun,
and the rainbows sigh
with the cries
of the stars in
            your eyes, my I's.
            your eyes, your I's.

UFO DREAMS

Thunder and rain,
I am beyond any pain.

A redemption paid.

Seagull flies high
in my inner divides.

Lighted triangle bright
illuminates unexpected
days and nights.

UFO dreams--
life is not what it seems--

Brambles and wine,
a cheap trick in summer time.

A stamp
on my passport
of yesteryear's wrath--
                        ironclad guards
laughing behind my back,

as my twisted shoulders
bud tendrils green,
unraveling datura vines
that trail down
my crooked seams.

Ashes to ashes,
dust to dust
sweep me away
on morrow's must.

Gift to the echoes,
promise to none--

                        I am no one
                        (I am you
                        and I am me)
                        branded by life's
                        slumberous dreams.

So halite I hail
as slow snails
sail,
puppy dog tales
are emptied into vomited pails.

Push deeper
the nails
            into my flesh--
                        let my blood stream.

Bluebird sings, angel wings--
    no martyrs here,

            a false promise of
                        an impossible dream.

Doe looks to me
so gentle and meek,
with arrow I will eat of her
(as Beast eats of me)
sucking out all that is
poisoned and
sweet.

EMERALD LOCKS

My parents
went away on a
fine ship of lilac lace:
a smile upon their faces
as they drifted out to sea.
The dolphins greeted them,
seal songs strong and walrus tusks.
They flowed on maple syrup currents
(sweet and ever full);
beams of stardust glistened on their sails.

Oh sail away, dear ones, for forever and a day.
Go and play, frolic in the new,
the new life, always awaiting you.

Be not afraid of the eagle and the spade.

Go gently into the night, beam bright on angel lights.

Go heal your souls of all these Earthly woes.

Sail away, sail away, on your pungent songs--
may they carry you along waterways to
emerald locks and crystal caves,
where your sea green
hair never dries,
and your spirit
never dies.

PAIN OF MY ANCESTORS

Fly away
pain of my Ancestors;
fly away from me.

Don't need to carry
your woes and travails.

Be gone now
        (in a way).
                Banish these aches and pains
                you carried while walking
                with your own two legs
        (that no longer exist)

See,

because of you,

I now persist.

            I am your spirit,
          the soul of your heart,
         your navel that traces
          the circumference
           of the Earth's
            equators

          that link us all
          in ways infinite
        and so very small.

Go now--
banished
from my realms
        of
        bumbled half-lives
        and crushing bone defeats--

Let's no longer fight for anything at all;
let me live in peace once and for all.

WEB OF LIES

Spider tells me
to weave a web of lies.
Deceptions and a tear,
make another cry.

Pain is good.

The universe is dark and dim.

There is no purpose here.

Two inch nails
go into my hide.
I have nowhere to hide,
the pain is all around me,
it is on all sides.

Carnelian comes calling,
bright red, a cheery one.
He tells me to have no fear
for the end of the world
is coming ever near.

And in this upside down time
when nothing makes any sense to me,
except a needle track and my cds,

I switch on a new
appliance, its energy hums
silently lighting up my artificial life,

as Spider weaves her web,
waiting patiently for this
curtain to come crashing down.

Coyote raises his snarly head,
filed teeth and a languid tongue.
Shaking a magic wand, he howls and
reassures that it is almost done;

While underfoot
the Termites
celebrate
by eating their feast of rotten wood,
and Butterflies run rampant
down sewaged alleys
and along strung out telephone poles.

Spider asks me,
"What will you weave in the morn?"

The curtain
it is closing on a tragic show
that will soon be moving out of town.

Burn bright, you bonfires of the night.

Bat wings,
teach me how to fly
and navigate the darkened
skies on sonic pulses and angel wings.

DEATH'S SONG

O You! How I long for you in all I say and do.

Your absence makes me strong,
as tinseled trees and corn leaves.

Your presence infuses me
with death's song,
that buzzes in my right ear,
as you speak to me of Hawaiian breezes and tropical trees,
hairy coconuts and places far away
that haunt us during our awake days.

O You! How I long for you in all I say and do.

And though your name is a mystery sublime,
a sound unutterable, a gift from the sand
    and temples divine--
on a mountaintop I stand
and consecrate this holy land
to:

O You! How I long for you in all I say and do.

David's star, Goliath's fight;
it has been such a long, long night.

Darkness seems everywhere.
My heart no longer beats
in syncopated rhymes
to the rhythms
of the stones and stars.

O You! How I long for you in all I say and do.

You are the breath
I cannot breathe,
all that I can never see,
you stand above and beyond
the blueberry bushes and eagle wings.

Cherry delights, holiday nights
with the candles alight.

O You! How I long for you in all I say and do.

A jasmine surprise, ghee in your eyes,
an elephant tusk, marigolds bright,
an alchemical tune to all unknown;
a shimmering blade of gypsum grass,
the clear crystal light beneath the moon bright.

Oh sunlight and stars, moonlight and dreams,
holy beams.

O You, How I long for you in all I say and do.

Help me to reawaken to a world anew,
enfolded in the chrysalis of my brittle heart's beat.

O You, How I long for you in all I say and do.

Peridot dreams, massive moonbeams--
A broken back.
I'll never come back,
so dream me on to a distant star
before you too are gone.

O You! How I long for you in all I do and say.

Cockroach cries to me, *smile is ecstasy.*
Nuclear pyres burning high
in our forever sky.

ROSE QUARTZ

Rose quartz, she knows.
Black-eyed susans do too--
what you once told me
before I knew you.

White corn burning bright
by the fire light.
Embers still glow,
what do you know
of once upon a time dreams
and fairy queens;
mermaid delights
and sugar puffed lives?

O Rose Quartz, she does know
with her glittery show
that it is by the mullein leaf wise
where the mushrooms do grow.

Murdered nights and slain days--
Oh save me, dear Rose Quartz,
by the river so wide
and may the eagle fly free,
not weighted down by you and me
and our impossible dreams of what can never be.

I lay down my sword, shining and bright--
let it be eclipsed by the deep moon's nights,
may it melt away in pyres of stars,
be engulfed by black holes and
timeless canyons of you.

I hold you now high,
looking up to the sky,
and ask for nothing at all--
I am ready to die

so something new can emerge
from the concrete and tired steel
of a civilization gone awry
on too much whiskey and zeal.

O Rose Quartz, let me mourn
this world so forlorn.

O Eagle,
guide me to
the tenderest tendrils
of what may one day be born.

O GUIDE

O Guide you are to me
and no one at all.

Your distant call,
so dim and imprecise,
like the poems I used to write and throw away
to hide them from the light of day.

O Guide you are to me,
I know not if you truly guide me
through all I do and see--
    labyrinths of enemies
    unexpected tunes
    scary sights
    torturers and gravity
    crying and poverty
    sickness all around...
        can no respite be found?

O Guide, come to me.

Help me to faintly see
the smallest whiff of who I am
as I nestle silent and alone,
my only true home.

O Guide, come to me.

Help me to truly see the beauty
of all this plight,
the meaning of this long night,

so I can share this message
with others yet to come
that I carry in my womb
now shriveled and too old.

O Guide, come to me.

O You, I can barely perceive.

Light my path,
show me the way
to honor you in all I do and say.

The bird sings,
gentle and sweet;
rainbowed sun rays,
my own heartbeat.

O Guide, bring to me
lapis dreams and velvet skies,
blueberry treats running down
my maple syruped thighs.

I raise a cup of nectar
to the promised ambrosia of our life,
dedicating myself to the activity
of merely staying alive.

O Guide, come to me,
O Guide beyond my dreams--

whisper to me of sweet nothings
that within me always reside.

O Guide, you come to me--
    the velvet hand
    the silver noose
    the golden goose,

the song unsung, the victory unwon,
    all I ever know undone--
        the rainbow bridge
           the cindered sun
           famed wine
                the promise of some-time.

INFINITE GRACE

I am a solitary soul,
this is my lonely fate,
and it is only in that deepest silence,
soft as velvet, gentle
as the feathered breath of eiderdown,
that I can faintly sense and feel
your presence ever close, forever near.

And in the din of daily life
with all its petty problems and mundane strife,
I search for your elusive face
only to find it in those rare flashes of infinite grace,
when time stands still and my mind's
winds cease to blow.

It is there in the quietude
that transcends all space
where I meet you (again):
Oh blessed one of infinite grace.

And to my bended knees I fall,
rejoicing in these fleeting, blessed moments
when I sense you radiant face
(in symbols that extend beyond infinite grace)
as you whisper revelations I can never fully perceive,
reassuring me I always will have just what I need.

And I so wish I could do more than be
simple, humble and sometimes confused me,
who doubts so many things,
except infinite grace.

HOLY ROCKS

Pomegranate eyes, smiles and a sigh.
Holy rocks, hazy praise
that lasts beyond all days.

Stifled songs in throats so wide;
nighttimes of bliss in neverness.

Domes of rocks
split open
to reach the skies and moons.

Sons of the sun
who worship the holy light
directly and thru no one.

Violet paths
to darkened caves
where prophets rage
about the evils of our days.

Simple one, child of the earth.
Salt and bone, eagle feather wide.

Turquoise skies
built by her hand divine
that needs nothing more
than simply you and me
when we make love
                or when we lay down to die--
    curled in a heap
        (a human garbage pile deep):

Ancestors of all time
 will you be mine?

Let my being entwine
with ageless wisdom
covered in animal hides
hidden in the crevices of waterfalls that
crash
through our minds,
releasing the poisons
we do unto ourselves
by worshipping pagan others
who think they know better
than we
that I am my own savior,
I am my own Messiah,
when you and I
kiss in our nakedness,
without any rules
 except to love to the extreme;
without any guidelines
 except those you whisper to me
  at first dawn
  when the light begins
  to infuse my own skies,
   giving me the power
   of the mysteries divine.

BLACK COHOSH EYES

Mandrake root, a faint sigh--
you and i
across the moon and millennia.

You reach out to me
with hands of motherwort
and black cohosh eyes,
bright with obsidian embers
of painted caves and caverns wide.

      (The mountain peak stands high,
    a sentinel, alone and distant from you and me.)

With burnished hands of steel
you ease my mind,
you cook my meals
   of millet and rice,
      amaranth and dandelion root.

Quinoa Man,
Sorghum Wife--
what kind of life
can we create as beings poised
between ecstasies of rivers wide?

Pointed point and rounded round--
ground to ground,
leaf and tree,
bird and bee.
    Honey wine, sweet nectar
        trickles my neck in ecstasy.

Corn to you,
you'll know what to do.

Mysteries of the stars divine.

Pathways to ecstasies unseen
                         to you and me.

Oh Star Beings that twinkle in your eyes.
Oh Earth Creatures of my ultimate domains--
passion's flames, burning nights,
sultry days of violet haze.

NOTHING KISS

My rock of Gibraltar
stands within me,
a perennial sentinel
deep in my see.

My grounding,
my mooring,
my task,
asking me
to try to be free,
when solid and strong
as a mountain stand I,
embraced by the forever sky
with roots in the waters
of you and me.

Tomorrow it may ask nothing
more than a nothing
kiss
engulfed in the infinite tinsel
of my nothingness.

ME

It just may be
that *me*
is a particle unsung,
a work undone, a fact unwon,
a gift unrealized and put to compost.

You
(who know me most),
pray tell what would you ever
see in *me*?

Hesitation
on the path.

Manifestation
of something yet to be.

Whispers
of the sounds,
when the sounds cease to exist.

The promise
of nothing
that can never be found.

I hesitate
before heaven's gate
can reveal its way
on this foggy and mundane day,
that is so bleak,
your words so meek,

your face so effortless,
your gifts all that I seek.

Oh come to me, come to me,
in the life I now lead--
caress me and teach me
how to conceive.

TREASURE

Hidden in the dew,
unbidden and away from your daily new,
a treasure enfolded in the now--
its gift is nothing
and it gives it all to you.

LEMMINGS LEAP

Towering cliffs,
a plunge in the dark;
the lemmings leap,
in my dreams go deep.

May I perchance sleep
til the end of time
and then awake sublime

in my newborn splendor
(that has yet to rot
even one spot)--

that is full blaze
of purple haze.

Stars weep
while we keep
a vigil silent, strong and deep,
for our Earth, upon whose breast
we always sleep.

My legs hurt.

My feet, I fear them not,
when pains erode the innards
of my brain.

I long for ultimate darkness,
but dim electricity
dulls my sight.

Oh dead of night,
O Dead of we--
May I asleep
til tomorrow's keep

and if I should die
before I awake
may I always know
that I am nothingness,
and unto that deep, purple void
I so long to go.

SWAN DIVE

Swan dive
into me.
Marbled dreams.
Ecstasy.

> I am rowing on dribbled dreams
> and moonbeams
> against the current
> and the currents
> that always surround me--
> my family,
> profound profanity.

> I am afraid
> I never loved You
> and yet I loved You
> too much--your touch--
> Ice maiden and Mother-wort.

The breast denied.
Acid wine, rancid milk,
curdled long before its time

as You and I danced the dance
of distance embraced--

our swan song sung
all our lives long
to emptied canyons of honeyed twines
woven in and out of our patterned lives.

THE ANCIENT ONES

Crack my back, make my stew,
help me create a world anew.

Mend my socks, tend my tears,
work the earth without remorse.

Pull the grass, plant the weeds,
nourish the trees and the bumble bees.

Bake the leavened bread with yeast that rises
from the ancient earth of long ago times.

Mash the wine with toes divine,
tingle with the blessings of the sweet earth sublime.

Cry out with joy for nothing at all.
Cry in the dead of night because you are a-light.

Fear not, my fearsome one,
the tale is still undone,
its ending yet to write,
so do not go gloomy into the night.

Rather rant and pant with full-bloodied cries
that you and I,
                        the Ancient Ones,
                                                are still alive--
in all these modern humans do and say,
we are just a hairbreadth away--
beyond the surf, within their dreams,
hidden in the most obvious places and seams.

WINGS OF DEATH'S DAY

I am ready to die, I know not why,
yet it seems to me I am ready to fly
far from this space, this place I reside--
been here for too long--
I've almost forgotten my stellar song.
So fly me away on the wings of death's day
into the bright light of your cosmic face.
Some fear what they don't know,
I fear more all I do behold
in this narrow land and time of such disgrace.
Guns and heroin needles,
no shame, lots of pain.
We can all be sold to the devil,
(which by the way doesn't exist,
except in our own realms we create for ourselves
to try to persist.)

Let me instead be like the grass, the rain and the dew,
that comes and is gone, then comes back anew.
Take me high, take me low,
take me to the cosmic place I have yet to know
where I may be embraced
by those of a kind and gentle face
as they whisper in my right ear (that no longer exists)
that it is time for me to no longer persist.

What a joy that will be when I come unto thee--
                              Mahogany of the heavens
                                Diamonds of the depths
                                  Salt of the heavens
                                    the Spider's web.

BANISH TOMORROW

The world can wait
while we let our love incubate.

Tell the President
I'll call him back tomorrow.

Check me out of work,
close the bedroom doors.

Let me touch your petals, peel your flesh,
lick your wounds, tend to your soul,
as you touch me with your moistened
lips of semen and dew,
in places known only to me and you.

The world can wait
while we let our love incubate.

Banish tomorrow,
live for the now.

Promise me your star
that hangs high in the sky
and entwines me with its songs
when you move me along
your rivers of you
and your slopes of now,
as the cherry blossoms sing
and the moon lights up the sun
in your forever sighs.

SEVEN YEAR MOURN

I dreamt
I was caught
in a box of tin-
foil and zebra hides.
Stripes beyond repair.
A downward swirl of acrid dust.

The turn of a stultifying
key that opened
other lifetimes
I should be living now.

Instead
I wallow
in the putrid mud
of my ancestors' last hurrah;

of my mother's gentle tears
(unbidden and unmoved)
that weave down yester-
years in rivulets of un-
marked graves;

as my father
tries to coax her
(unsuccessfully, I may add)
to smile at the rainbow's
rains
that shatter our lives
like an arrow-
head from ancient times,

as rivulets of muddied tears
drip down her giraffed neck:
spotted with the for-
ever dis-illusions
of mother-hood's
suffocating
sounds

and

I am just a pin-
prick of yellowing reminders
that once upon a time
they loved
before their breaths
became my dust.

Oh hark to yester-
years when no one
knew how to mourn.

On a distant seven-year morn
full of grief,
when the lock
turned
and my boxes
tautened into leathered steel,
as stolen times and wide glances
prance along lifetimes
lost to nothingness.

BLESS ME

O Child of the Earth,
O Child of pagan birth,
Oh corn and straw, oh silky hair divine--
Bless me in my summertime.

Bless me in my passions,
bless me in my grace,
bless me when I stumble
and lose your holy face.

Bless me when I'm wrong,
bless me when I'm meek,
bless me when I'm scared
of the silent words I sometimes hear you speak.

Bless me when others try to call
the devils back to this earth again.
Bless all who walk the light-filled path,
brushing away debris for others yet to come.

Bless me when I've been wronged, or so I humbly think.
Bless me to realize that no matter what happens,
it's only a single chapter in times
too infinite to ever comprehend.

Bless me when I grapple with things I can't understand.
Bless me when I'm silent and can faintly feel your hand,
holding mine so firmly, invisible and strong.

Help me when I have enough to stop and share;
digging deep into my pockets that have dust and lint,

spreading out the wisdom wealth
like sowing crops upon a newly laid field.

Help me when I ache,
help me with my pains,
help me with the fogginess
that sometimes creeps into my heart and brain.

Help me, O Messiah,
who has always walked upon this Earth,
hidden in the earth, enshrined in stones and tides.

Help me to unravel mysteries wide
before I lay me down to die.

GARDEN OF MY SOUL

Oh garden of my soul,
I feel I am growing old.
My hair, she turns white.
My teeth, they no longer bite
into morsels of human flesh
offered to my amazingness.

Don't hate me, my child,
for I am of the ancient times
when covenants wide
nourished all our lifetimes.

Now stand in your nakedness--
rounded breast and painted penis--
on mountaintops where bluebirds extol
the intricate designs of your eternal soul.

Harken to the angels,
the angels of your own heart,
that sing to you of the sweetness you can impart
when in ceremonies true
given from the heart of you
you offer your soul
to those of us who are growing old.

Step forward, my child, child of my flesh.
Step forward, young man, and take up the yoke
of society's mores we humans are brought
here to amend, with an amen
from our innards
given with the voices of all times

that shelter us in their harbors
of smooth Turkish delights.

My feet they are weak,
my muscles strain and toil
to understand this time and place
which seems to me to have such an ugly human face.

And when I lay me down to die,
perhaps you learn then, my child,
that I was truly your Messiah wise.

THE NEXT MESSIAH

Rejoice for the next Messiah
has already been born.

He is in the bushes, she is in the bees;
it resides all around us in all you do and see.

It resides within us
when daylight is gone
and night she does arrive.

Pine trees, tell me who you are.
Cypress blessed by a distant star.
Hemlock and spruce, the redwoods too,
speak the blood of Christ that flows like sweet sap
through each and every one of our lives.

Oh gazelle, fleet of foot,
Oh Dead Sea, deep and salty,
Oh grain of sand, in which quartz hidden doth reside.

You are all my sacred brides
to whom I offer my ultimate sacrifice
                                    of no sacrifice at all.

I do not believe our next Messiah
will tell us we need to spill blood to be free.

I AM OPEN

I am open to what Spirit has to bring:
                              on bird wing,
                              from the butterfly,
                              on a cloud of mist,
                              in my child's cries.

I am open to what Spirit has to sing:
                              on my sighs,
                              on my good-byes...
that welcome in a tomorrow of which I am still blind.

I am open to what Spirit is,
(if it is anything):
                              Mother Earth
                              Father Sky,
                              all and nothing...
the hollow ice of remembrance
housed in my spleen.

I am open to what I can rarely glean
of stars and dust,
Earth and my musts--

passions aborted   path's unturned.

I am open to yesteryears
which my ancestors walked with care,
    tousling my unborn hair
    with their salty dreams of me.

Oh yes, I am open
to what spirit move in me:
                        (heart and liver)
                                (ear and tongue);
                        licking diamond wounds
                        with feathered yarrow wands;

Eating at the table
never set for me,

('cause I'm still looking for Spirit
                                outside me in the breeze).

Until I finally crash and fall,
welcoming the Spirit
that never
knows me at all:
                        the hand unclapped,
                        eyes closed wide,
                        belly buttons unraveling,
                        I am coming home to die

as stone to steel
and earth to meal
are marked on mountain tops
for all the winds to heal.

You are finished now,
this book you may close and put away.
Perhaps you will take it up once again another day.

Thank you for visiting these Spirit Songs--
no matter where you live, what you look like,
what your life, we are forever united now--
two sparks that light up this Mystic Morn,
bound hand and hand and heart to heart.

Stone dust to star dust,
rainbow skies and quetzal eyes,
the winged serpent raises its scaly head
breathing purple flames of wisdom bright,
swirling clouds of violet haze.

Blessing to you and your loved ones
for all of your days.

www.ingramcontent.com/pod-product-compliance
Lightning Source LLC
LaVergne TN
LVHW041206080426
835508LV00008B/832